Table of
Contents

What Is Severe Weather?

Sometimes calm weather turns **violent**. Storms roll in and bring **severe** weather.

Thunder booms and **lightning** flashes. Lightning bolts can be dangerous. Sometimes they strike the ground.

Funnel clouds can appear during a thunderstorm. They become **tornadoes** if they touch down.

The swirling winds
can rip apart houses
and move trees.

Some thunderstorms bring too much rain. They can cause floods.

Lakes and rivers cannot hold
the rain. Water covers roads.
Basements take in water.

Some thunderstorms start over the ocean. They often become **hurricanes**.

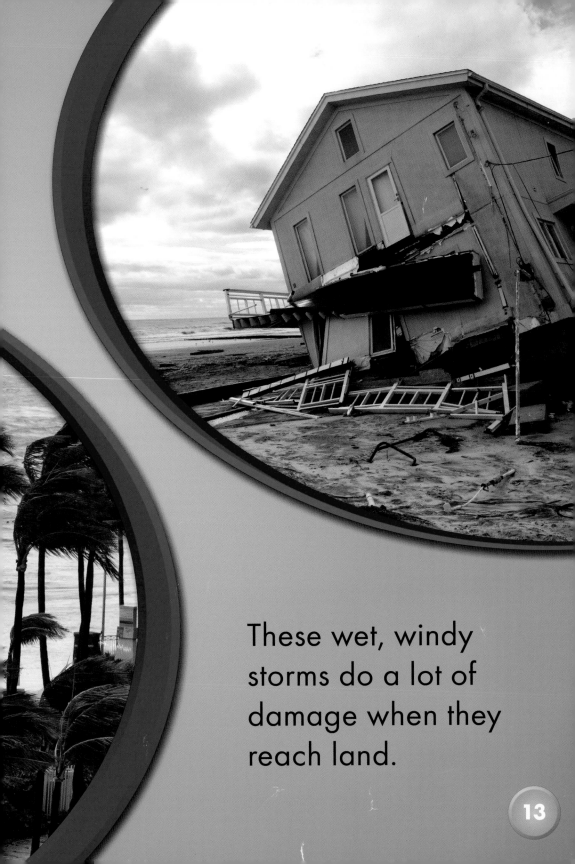

These wet, windy storms do a lot of damage when they reach land.

In cold weather, severe storms bring blowing snow. They are called **blizzards**.

Strong winds cause **whiteouts**. Driving becomes dangerous.

Tracking Severe Weather

Severe weather scares
many people.

Other people like to watch storms. Some even become **storm chasers**.

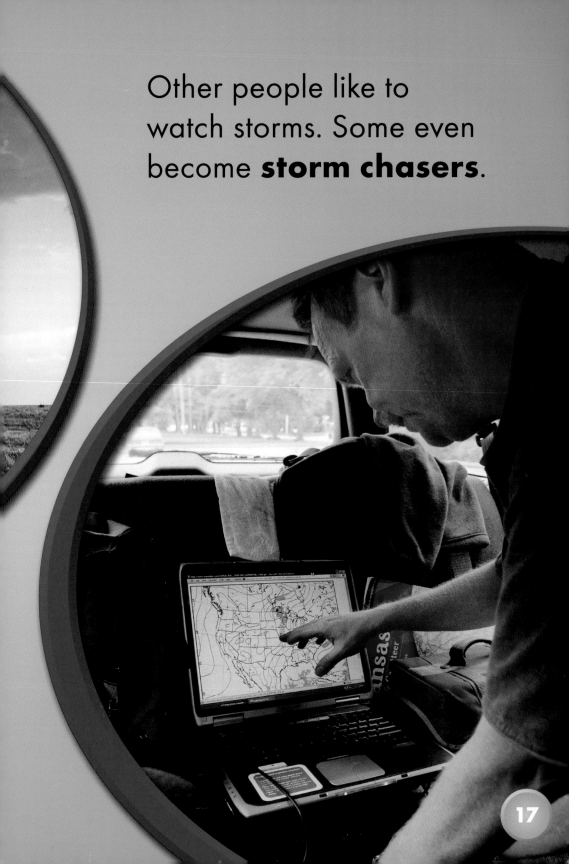

Meteorologists use **satellites** and **radar** to track severe weather.

satellites

radar

They issue a watch if conditions are right for a storm.

They issue a warning if a storm is reported.

STORMTRACKER RADAR

SEVERE THUNDERSTORM WARNING

February 20 - 7:20 PM

Kansas City

Mark Twain
National Fore

Ozark National
Forest

KANSAS

orest

This means the storm is close or in the area. It is time to get to a safe place!

Glossary

blizzards—heavy snowstorms with strong winds

flood—to cover usually dry land with water

funnel clouds—spinning clouds that turn into tornadoes if they touch the ground

hurricanes—huge storms with swirling winds that start over the ocean

lightning—an electric spark in the sky

meteorologists—people who study and predict the weather

radar—a tool that sends out radio waves to collect weather data

satellites—tools that move around in space to collect weather data

severe—strong and harmful

storm chasers—people who follow storms

thunder—a loud noise that goes with lightning

tornadoes—funnel clouds that touch down on the ground

violent—forceful and able to cause harm

whiteouts—when blowing snow makes seeing difficult

To Learn More

AT THE LIBRARY

Boothroyd, Jennifer. *What Is Severe Weather?* Minneapolis, Minn.: Lerner Publications Company, 2015.

Tieck, Sarah. *Storm Chasers*. Edina, Minn.: ABDO Pub. Co., 2012.

Wiesner, David. *Hurricane*. New York, N.Y.: Clarion Books, 2008.

ON THE WEB

Learning more about severe weather is as easy as 1, 2, 3.

1. Go to www.factsurfer.com.

2. Enter "severe weather" into the search box.

3. Click the "Surf" button and you will see a list of related web sites.

With factsurfer.com, finding more information is just a click away.

Index